Asians in Britain

A Christian Understanding

Patrick Sookhdeo

Exeter: The Paternoster Press

ISBN: 0 85364 207 9
Copyright © The Paternoster Press Ltd., 1977

AUSTRALIA
Emu Book Agencies Pty., Ltd.,
63 Berry Street, Granville, N.S.W., 2142

SOUTH AFRICA
Oxford University Press
P.O. Box 1141, Oxford House,
11, Buitencingle Street, Cape Town

Typeset by Input Typesetting Ltd., London and printed in
Great Britain by Butler and Tanner for The Paternoster
Press Ltd., Paternoster House, 3 Mount Radford Crescent,
Exeter, Devon.

Contents

One
A problem or a responsibility?

The arrival of Asians – Muslims, Sikhs, Hindus and Buddhists –
in Britain is experienced by many people as a problem or as a
threat to the type of existence they have idealised for themselves.
Others see it as a responsibility obligating this country to offer a
better standard of living to these people. Christians, however,
should interpret it as a God-given opportunity. As Christians we
are called upon to serve our Lord by proclaiming the Gospel to all
men everywhere, so the arrival of many adherents of other
religions on our doorsteps should be seen as a great opportunity
for sharing the love of Christ with those who have not yet heard.

Before the second world war almost all approaches to the great
world religions by Christians were made from a position of
superiority or arrogance. We were always right, others wrong.
Our religious system held all the answers, others had nothing
worthwhile within them from which we could learn. We were
god-fearing, they were pagan and heathen. Inevitably such attitudes led to conflict with the followers of other religions, and
often they tended to link Christianity with the ruling power.

In this more enlightened day, however, the situation has changed considerably. Christians are being made aware of the many vir-
tues and ideals contained in other religions. Examples of this
would be the Muslim's ethic, discipline and concept of God; the
Hindu's spirituality and intense activity to know God; the
Buddhist's self-denial and self-discipline; and the Sikh's love and
devotion and amazing tolerance. There is much that the Christian
can learn from these religions, particularly in the realms of
behaviour and devotion.

However, though such an attitude should lead to greater
tolerance, understanding and compassion for those of other faiths,
it must not lead to syncretistic and universalist tendencies on our
part. The Christian faith teaches the uniqueness of Christ as
God's full and final revelation to man, and as the only way to
God. In Christ we see the embodiment of all that other faiths seek.
The Muslim's ethic is displayed in the character and life of Jesus;
and the Hindu's spirituality in the constant communion of Jesus

with the Father. The Buddhist's self-denial is seen in the
sacrificial and dedicated life of our Lord, and the Sikh's love,
devotion and service in him whose name is love and who served
man to the uttermost, even in giving his life on the cross.

As Christians we have a duty and a responsibility to present the
saving and reconciling work of Christ to all men, of whatever
faith. But it must be done with humility and understanding, love,
and most of all with the gentle and meek spirit of our Master.

In presenting the Gospel we need to listen to what the other person is saying, and to understand the full impact of his religion
upon his life and thoughts. We should not be negative in our approach, demolishing the other person's religion; but positive,
presenting the Christ whom we trust and have experienced, the
Lord who has revealed himself to us. As our Lord loved us and
saved us, so we are to demonstrate a similar love in our service to
those of other faiths. Compassion and not argument is to be our
motive.

The following chapters give a brief introduction to the
background, culture and beliefs of these Asian immigrants. In the
main they give only general statements, because of the need for
brevity. For those who wish to go further into the subject, a
booklist is provided at the end.

THE ASIAN COMMUNITY: SOME POINTS TO CONSIDER

Diverse Background

What makes up the Asian community in Britain? It is easy to
speak of it *en bloc* without true regard to the many and varied
differences within the community. The Asian community is made
up of Pakistanis, people from Bangladesh, Indians from the
Punjab, Gujarat, other parts of India and East Africa. All are as
different from each other as the Englishman is from them. So in
our relationships with them we need to know their backgrounds,
religions and cultures, before we can effectively gain a working
relationship with them and overcome the many misunderstandings
which can occur. Above all they are to be treated as individuals,
and not just as 'Indians' or 'Pakistanis'.

What then are the main communities in Britain? The majority
of Indians come from two areas – Punjab and Gujarat. They
speak the languages Punjabi, Hindi and Gujarati, and their
religions are Sikhism and Hinduism. The people from Bangla-

desh and Pakistan speak Bengali or Urdu, and their religion is Islam. Each of these ethnic groups can often be identified by physical features such as skin colour and bone structure.

The person from Bangladesh tends to be of small, fine stature with quite a dark skin. The Punjabi is of a more stocky build with a paler skin. There is a tendency towards European features indicative of the ancestry. With experience comes the ability to distinguish the various peoples.

Dress, especially the women's, is a guide to the country of origin. The Punjabi or Sikh women wear a pyjama-type outfit. The *salwar* or trousers are wide at the waist, and narrow at the bottom. The shirt is termed a *kamiz*. The Pakistani woman wears a similar type of clothing except that the trousers are narrow at the knees and often flared at the bottom. Gujarati women will frequently wear a sari in one of a number of styles. The important factor for Asian women is that their dress does not define their physical features, and that they are well covered. This meets religious as well as social sanctions. Thus the anglicizing of women as far as dress is concerned is not encouraged. The red spot worn by many women, once a caste mark, is often used by both single and married women for decorative purposes.

Most of the men wear Western clothes. Only the Sikh is distinguishable by his turban, usually neat and immaculate, and in any colour. The wearing of headgear by Asians is regarded as a mark of respect, and it is worn indoors as well as out of doors, for example in mosques and temples.

Difficulties Encountered

The majority of Asians come from a rural background where they were predominantly farmers. One of the many difficulties that such people face is the upheaval of moving from a rural environment to an urban and highly industrialized society. Besides this emotional upheaval there is the moral conflict caused when conservative and semi-Victorian attitudes come face to face with the relatively permissive, free-for-all society of Britain. Further difficulties arise as men find their skills and trades unsuitable and redundant in this new society. However the past few years have seen the arrival of many Asians with a high degree of education, such as doctors, teachers and engineers, who do not share the problems to the same extent. They do face others when their qualifications are not accepted and so they are prevented from taking positions at the level they had expected.

Stabilizing Factors

The Asian is fortunate in that he takes his culture with him wherever he goes. This is one of the stabilizing factors that can counter emotional and other upheavals. Perhaps it finds best expression in the concept of the 'extended family': this consists of all the members of a family of all generations in the male line, who live communally sharing everything. When marriage takes place the family is extended even further, until a 'village kin' group is formed. Therefore a bond of comradeship between members of a village is formed, and relationships strengthened. It is from among this 'extended family' in Britain that the Asian finds his relatives, friends, sponsors, advisors and helpers. Though they may be spread all over Britain, contacts with each other are maintained by personal visits where a bed, food and welcome are never refused. The Asian is not left entirely alone to face his new-found problems, as there are always others with whom he can share them.

Another stabilizing factor is to be found within the community spirit of the Asian. Unlike the Western concept of the individual as the basic unit in society, the Asian stresses the family, as is demonstrated in the 'extended family'. To quote an Indian writer,

> 'Most people in the villages in India are very friendly and hospitable and they lead a communal life. Their doors are always open to their friends and relations, and when relations come to stay with them there is naturally a little overcrowding. They don't feel that this is wrong in any way. In fact Indians have a positive duty to relations to put them up.'

The Indians and Pakistanis are also a very religious people. Almost every part of their lives revolves around some aspect of religion. Thus when considering the behaviour and attitude of the Asian, one needs to take into account his religion and religious background.

The position of men

In the extended family the eldest male holds the most important position. However, in Britain, the father, or the eldest male member in this country, takes this position, although certain problems are still resolved in India or Pakistan. The father's position is one of both authority and respect, and is also a source of stability. He makes the decisions that affect the family, though matters are usually shared by both husband and wife. For example, when a health visitor calls on the family, she is usually taken to see the husband, who makes any decisions considered necessary.

The position of women

It is important to distinguish here between the uneducated families, who tend to be more conservative, and the educated families who are more liberal in their outlook. Amongst the former, wives often do not eat until after the men have eaten. The practice of women walking three paces behind their husbands is occasionally seen. The majority of women are confined to the home. Because they are unable to understand English or read, even in their own language, they are shy and sensitive. It is interesting to note that though the women may seem to hold a subordinate position, this is because of the function they fulfil in the home, rather than the fact that they are women. Guru Nanak, the founder of Sikhism, said, 'How can they (women) be regarded as inferior when they give birth to the greatest of men?' Another Guru wrote, 'Women are the conscience of men.' For the Muslims there is a Pakistani saying, 'If you are seeking for heaven, look for it under your mother's feet.' Thus the woman's status in the home as wife and mother commands respect.

Marriage

The majority of Asians still practise 'arranged marriage'. In other words the initiative is taken by the parents in finding an appropriate partner for their son or daughter, and this often leads to conflict. However, today, young people do have some say in the matter. According to the Asian, in the West, 'you fall in love, marry, and repent at leisure', but for him it is 'you marry then fall in love'. In this way there is less chance of disillusionment. For the Asian the concept of platonic friendships between members of the opposite sex is practically unknown, except for the very educated or liberal. Thus the friendliness and openness of English women can lead to grave misunderstandings with Asian men. In the areas where there is a predominantly male Asian population, often the only type of English women they meet are prostitutes. So they can get the impression that most English women are like this. Thus when evangelizing it is essential that women go to the women and men to the men.

Children

It is with the children that the most serious difficulties are encountered. As most Asian mothers do not speak English, children of pre-school age are generally brought up without any knowledge of the English language. Also they have not had the opportunity of entering into the particular thought forms and play activities that English children engage in before going to school. On entering primary schools this can prove to be a great handicap. Perhaps the answer lies in the use of play groups and nursery schools for such children.

At secondary school level, what can be termed the 'conflict of culture' begins. At home the Asian youngster is brought up in an Indo-Pakistani culture, where he speaks his native language and eats his own particular kind of food. However, at school, he enters the English environment in which he is equally expected to share. He lives and moves in two opposing cultures, each having a drawing effect on him. This occurs particularly in the field of morality, where he goes from the strict code of ethics in the home to the freer morals of the school and society.

On the effects of integration a Muslim wrote recently, 'The biggest danger confronting Muslims, is that children grow up not knowing about their own religion and history, thinking themselves English, but when they leave school disillusionment sets in and they are neither English nor Pakistani, neither Christian nor Muslim, rootless like the Negro youth in the USA cities'.

To lessen this disillusionment children usually undergo instruction in their particular language and religion for a few hours after school and on Saturdays and Sundays. This can total up to twelve hours a week. Speaking of girls in particular, an English writer says, 'Problems arise, however, in this country, where children, especially girls, have grown up with one foot in our culture and imbibed Western ideas of personal freedom and permissiveness through primary and secondary education. Cases of deep rebellion and deep tension are growing. A custom which is valid in an environment where it is universally practised, is very hard to enforce where other girls, the majority, are clearly seen to live entirely differently, and many uneducated Asian parents do not fully make allowances for the overwhelming pressures on their teenagers.' Help needs to be given to both parents and children to help them overcome these difficulties.

Other problems affecting children lie in the realms of dress, diet and religious customs. Since the Asian stresses purity, dress for the girls is expected to cover all parts of the body. This can lead to difficulties with the school authorities over school uniforms and in games where girls are expected to change into shorts or swim suits.

Food also presents a problem, as each religion has its own prohibitions. Most Hindus do not eat meat because they believe in the sanctity of all living things; Muslims do not eat pork, because they, like Jews, regard the pig as an unclean animal. Sikhs can eat meat but some refuse beef in particular lest they offend Hindus; Sikhs and Muslims will eat only meat ritually killed by their own butchers. Because of uncertainty about the food set before them, children will often refuse to eat it.

Muslim and Hindu children are expected to carry out the fasts prescribed by their religion. For the Muslim child this means fasting for one month of the year from sunrise until sunset. This can lead to a child getting irritable through lack of food. Because of the demands of their religion, children are singled out as different from English children, sometimes leading to isolation with the resultant loneliness. This is well demonstrated by the wearing of turbans by the Sikh boys. Older boys and girls are not expected to mix socially with each other. This can lead to parents withdrawing their children from activities where the sexes intermingle. For this reason youth clubs on the whole have been unsuccessful in attracting Asian girls. However, boys are allowed a greater degree of freedom.

Health

The majority of orthodox Hindus eat neither meat nor eggs. This lack of protein can lead to dietary deficiencies. The lack of sunshine can lead to vitamin D deficiency. As many Asian mothers and children spend most of their time indoors, they become very susceptible to respiratory infections. In some areas severe anaemia is the most common problem. Nervous illnesses amongst women are on the increase because of the many pressures encountered in Britain. Often midwives are concerned when Muslim women ask to have their babies' heads shaved after birth. This is a symbolic taking away of the uncleanness of birth, as well as to help the hair grow in greater profusion. Circumcision is obligatory for male Muslim children. It is normally performed a few days after birth, but can be carried out up to the age of eight.

Work

The fact that many of the Asians come from a rural agricultural background has meant that their skills have become superfluous in this country. Therefore they have to take unskilled and semi-skilled jobs that no one else wants. For qualified Asians their problem has been one of recognition. On the whole their qualifications have not been acceptable.

Problems can occur in industry over dress, language, habits, hygiene, food, and the religious observance of certain holidays. Sikhs in particular would object to wearing headgear other than their turbans or to the total removal of them (although they may be removed for games). To some it may seem petty, but to the Sikh the turban is of fundamental importance since it is required by his religion as one of the outward expressions of his faith.

As with children, food presents a great problem. This has been discussed above. Like the Jews, Asians have religious festivals which mean being away from work. The two principal Muslim feasts, which have religious as well as social importance, are the Breaking of the Fast at the end of the month of Ramadan, and the Sacrifice of the Pilgrimage. All work is normally stopped on these two days. Muslim workers will therefore stay away from work unless given authorized holidays, to carry out their religious duties. It would be useful if employers would discuss with their Asian employees the dates of their main festivals and arrange for them to have these days off, rather than waiting until no one shows up for work. However the majority of Hindus and Sikhs in England celebrate particular festivals on the nearest Sunday so their working week is not disturbed.

Conclusion

In considering these cultural practices we need to heed Chesterton's wise remark, 'Don't take the front gate down until you know why the previous owner put it up'. In other words, it is unwise to try to change a cultural practice unless you fully understand why it existed in the culture in the first place.

Finally, we need to remember that people caught in the disorganizing effects of rapid change – rural, social, cultural and moral – require not less understanding but more. It is necessary to gain an insight into the meaning this experience has for the Asian who is caught in the middle of it. This should lead to respect for the Asian who is experiencing this change, and not just to the imposition of another life upon him. Communication flows from an awareness of what things mean to him rather than what they mean to us.

It is here that the Christian can play an important role. Asians in Britain need love and compassion. Christians believe that they are in touch with the source of *all* love and *all* compassion and that in Jesus Christ they have experienced the *agape* of God, his selfless and self-giving love expressed in Jesus Christ. It is in compassion and concern, derived from him, that he can most effectively be made real to other people. Christian love will speak to the heart of the Asian in sharp contrast to the rejection which he so often experiences.

Two
Hinduism

Hinduism has been described as a rich jungle which has grown and spread in tropical profusion. It can lay no claim to any historical founder, central authority, institutional organization or creed. It is a mixture of philosophy, ritual, ancient customs and traditions. India is the stronghold of Hinduism where there are some 500 million followers. Indian migrants have taken Hinduism into many countries, for example East Africa, Malaysia and Great Britain. In Britain the majority of Hindus are from the Gujarat state in the North West of India.

The origin of Hinduism

Hinduism has been regarded as the oldest religion in the world. Its history goes back almost 5,000 years when the fair-skinned Aryan invaders poured into N.W. India from Europe, and conquered the darker Dravidians who were pushed into south India. To this day the difference in colour and physique can still be seen.

The Aryans then established a strong rural society, which gave the cow a prominent place because of the important commodities it provided. This may be the original reason why the cow was revered and worshipped. The Aryans also tended to ponder on the nature of the universe, its greatness and comprehensiveness. The ideas carried on by tradition for many years were eventually written down, forming the Hindu literature of today.

Hindu Religious Literature

Hindu scriptures are divided into two classes: *Sruti* and *Smriti*.

1. *Sruti* ('that which is heard')
The *Sruti* is made up of the four Vedas which are the primary sources and authoritative texts of Hinduism. The four Vedas are the Rig-Veda, the Sama-Veda, the Yajur-Veda and the Atharva-Veda. Each of these consist of four main parts:
  (i) the *Mantras*: the hymns and chants in praise of God.

(ii) the *Brahmanas*: explanations of the mantras, together with detailed descriptions of the sacrificial rites.

(iii) the *Aranyakas*: meditations on the symbolic meanings of the sacrifices.

(iv) the *Upanishads*: these go beyond ritual to discuss the nature of the universe and man's relation to it. The teachings of the Upanishads are known as *Vedanta* – the *anta* or end of the Veda.

2. *Smriti* ('that which is remembered')

All scriptures other than the Vedas are known as *Smriti*. They include many stories and legends and rules for conduct. The two most noteable ones are the *Puranas* (the great epics) – the *Ramayana* and the *Mahabharata*.

(i) *Ramayana*

This is the story of Rama who destroys the demon-king Ravana and re-establishes righteousness on earth. Rama is believed to be an incarnation of God and the repetition of his name is the most common devotional exercise in popular Hinduism.

(ii) *Mahabharata*

This is the story of a great war between the hundred *Kaurava* brothers, who represent Evil, and the five cousins, the *Pandavas*, who represent Good. With the help of Sri Krishna, another incarnation of God, Good triumphs over Evil.

The *Bhagavad Gita* is the best known book of Hindu scriptures and is a part of the *Mahabharata*. It is regarded by many as the Hindu Bible and teaches men to do their duty which is based on the need for selfless action as a result of an unfailing devotion to God.

Some beliefs of the Hindu

1 *His view of God*

(i) Animism

The early Aryans were animists, that is the gods to whom their worship and sacrifice were offered were the powers of nature. There were gods of heaven, of thunder, of fire. These and many other gods were the powers supreme over human destiny, whose wrath must be averted, and whose favour must be won by sacrifices, magic incantations, and hymns of praise. They were similar to the gods of European mythology. In the course of time, the belief in nature gods began to decay because their worship was found to be deficient. It was felt that there must be an ultimate reality at the heart of all things, and this gave rise to philosophical speculation.

(*ii*) Monism

In their quest they came to the belief that there was only one force in the universe. This force, the supreme power, they termed Brahman (a neuter word not to be confused with the term Brahmin which referred to a member of the priestly caste), which was beyond all thought and language, beyond all conditions and attributes. Thus Brahman is indescribable and can be termed *it, being, intelligence, bliss.* All things are said to be part of Brahman, so that there is no personal existence or identity. All things around us are merely an illusion. As one Hindu book puts it, 'Brahman alone is real'.

Against this philosophical speculation, a few centuries before the Christian era there arose a concept of God that regarded him as a person, one who was interested in the day to day affairs of man. This was similar to the Jewish and Christian concept of God. Probably it arose as a protest by the ordinary man against the cold intellectualism of abstract philosophy. His heart yearned for one to whom he could pray and with whom he could communicate.

(*iii*) Polytheism

This is the belief in and worship of many gods. At the centre of this is the *Trimurti*, composed of three separate gods:

(a) Brahmā – the creator
(b) Vishnu – the preserver
(c) Shiva – the destroyer and reproducer of life

Each of the three gods of the *Trimurti* had a wife and children. This resulted in a number of deities, all of whom could be worshipped.

The god Vishnu was said to have come down to earth from time to time in various incarnations or avataras. The Bhagavad Gita says, 'Whenever there is a decay of Dharma (religion and righteousness) and a growth of irreligion, then I do send myself forth. From age to age I am incarnate to save the good, to destroy evil-doers, and to establish Dharma'.

There are said to be ten such incarnations which Vishnu assumed to save mankind, and these include taking the forms of animals, sub-human, and human forms. The two most popular are Rama and Krishna. The tenth incarnation is yet to come, and then he will appear as a victorious messiah, mounted on a white horse, with a flaming sword in his hand.

(*iv*) Monotheism
Akin to polytheism but on a higher level, there then emerged the belief that there was only one god, who is personal, who desires our love, to whom we can pray, and sometimes coming very near to the Christian view of God, although it is still viewed in the context of Hindu monistic pantheism.

2 His view of man
In general the Hindu regards man as having no separate identity from god. God (Brahman) is seen to be everywhere, and to exist in all things. Thus man is simply a part of god, and god and man are regarded as the same. To the Hindu the world around is unreal. This *maya* or illusion that the world is real is conceived as a film of ignorance clouding our vision, so we imagine the material world around us to be real, and are blind to spiritual reality. From the Christian point of view it is possible to conceive *maya* not as a film of ignorance clouding our vision, but as sin which separates us from God. We hold that the world around us is a real world, but because of sin we are separated from the spiritual realm.

3 Salvation
Within salvation there are two important factors:

(*i*) Reincarnation
The Hindu believes that all life is a continual struggle to bring oneself into perfect union with Brahman. Life is a wheel of birth, death, and rebirth from which one seeks liberation. Thousands of births are necessary before union. Behaviour in one life is rewarded or punished in the next. Bad deeds take one further away from union, and good deeds lead one nearer. Life is like an ever-rolling wheel with no beginning and no end. This cycle of rebirths is called *Samsara*.

(*ii*) Karma
The Hindu believes, 'What you sow you reap'. Each new birth into which the Hindu comes is determined by *karma*, the deeds determining one's destiny. His deeds in this life determine the type of life he will have in the next existence. By good living he may be reborn into a higher state in the next life. By bad living he can

worsen his state. It is all dependent on works.

Salvation for the Hindu is the stopping of this endless cycle of death and rebirth, release from the wheel of *samsara*. This is said to occur when a person recognizes that the world around him is an illusion, that he has no separate existence, but that he is part of Brahman. This liberation or merging with the one is called *moksha*. There are three ways of achieving this, which could be termed three ways of salvation. They are:

(*i*) The path of knowledge or meditation, called *jnana mārga*.
This is the most difficult. It is control over the body, leading to control over the mind, leading to control over the spirit. This involves Yoga, not as a series of exercises as is the Western concept, but rather as an abstract way of freeing oneself from all earth-binding desires through control of the bodily system, to such an extent that attainment with the 'it', the 'infinite' is achieved. The result is that one's desires are controlled, and no new round of *karma* begins.

(*ii*) The path of works or deeds, called *karma mārga*.
This does not admit of the sudden liberation of the *jnana mārga*, but should lead to steady progress up the ladder of life. Doing good works means building sufficient *karma* to obtain release from *samsara*.

(*iii*) The path of devotion, called *bhakti mārga*.
This is the most popular way, involving much love and adoration for Vishnu and his incarnations, Krishna and Rama.

4 Death

Death to the Hindu is just another step into a new life, so he does not care for particulars or ceremony at death. The body is cremated and the ashes are scattered with the words of the Brahmin, 'He goes to where he comes from.'

During this life the Hindu accumulates good or bad *karma* which determine the state of the new body or mind. If the *karma* of this life is bad, then he will be reincarnated in a lower form; if the *karma* is good then the nature of the new life will be better. The Hindu seeks liberation from the cycle of rebirths (*samsara*), so looks upon death as just another stage in the endless cycle.

5 The end of life

Hindus believe that once the soul obtains release it is absorbed into the ultimate where it ceases to exist. It becomes part of the all. Thus there is neither heaven nor hell in Hinduism.

Castes

Hindus believe that the castes originated from the body of Brahmā, the personalized form of Brahman, the Godhead. The four castes are:

(*i*) Brahmins – priests – springing from the head of Brahmā

(*ii*) Kshatriyas – warriors – springing from the shoulders of Brahmā

(*iii*) Vaisyas – businessmen, professionals, traders – springing from the thighs of Brahmā

(*iv*) Sudras – labourers – springing from the feet of Brahmā

A fifth group comprised the so-called outcastes, or people who did not belong to any of these four categories. The outcaste people or untouchables are said to be 'under his feet'. This caste developed between the first and second century BC, and is sometimes referred to as the Candala caste. These people were outcastes through crime or social misdemeanour, and were given tasks such as dealing with animal flesh, cleaning toilets etc.

The caste system is now outlawed by Indian constitutional law, but social changes cannot happen overnight, and as the system is so deeply ingrained in Indian society, it still has importance in many areas.

Hindu Worship

1 In the home

There is no definite practice for every Hindu to perform, therefore worship is very much an individual matter. Sometimes on the mantelshelf of an English fireplace will be a picture of Shiva or Krishna, or a highly coloured picture serving as a household god or shrine. This could be surrounded by flowers and incense. Prayers will be said facing the god, with hands together in a *namaste* or greeting position.

Children are taught to read from the Gita at a very early age. The Gita is read aloud daily, and mothers teach their children how to worship gods at home. The mother thus plays a very important part in the training of Hindu children.

In any home a visit from a *guru* or spiritual teacher would be welcomed.

An orthodox Hindu wakens early, bathes, then says prayers. Of all the prayers the Gayatri Mantra is as familiar and as necessary to the Hindu as the Lord's prayer to the Christian. It is chanted at all Hindu ceremonies, at birth, marriage, and formal openings. Basically it is worship of the Sun as a manifestation of god known as *Savitri*.

2 In the temple

In Britain temples have been established in most places where there is a Hindu community. A house may be adopted, or a church once used for Christian worship. Before entering, shoes must be removed. Inside, the temple is highly coloured and decorative, containing shrines of gods and goddesses. A temple is usually frequented more by women than by men. Women visit frequently to make their prayers and offerings or to secure some favour. There is no set form of worship, each family following its own pattern, which can have ancestral implications. Music is considered a most essential part of reaching out to god in worship. The creative arts have been harnessed in Hindu worship, and now music, sculpture, dance and drama are considered religious rather than secular in inspiration. There are set times when the gods and goddesses are woken up ceremoniously and fed on saffron coloured rice. This is accompanied by bell ringing, incense and loud classical music.

Stages in the Hindu life

According to the Hindu, life is divided into four stages:
  (*i*) Brahmacharya – discipline, chastity, education
  (*ii*) Grihasthiya – householder, family life
  (*iii*) Vanaprastha – retreat from household ties
  (*iv*) Sanyasa – complete renunciation of the world.
Each period of life has a religious significance. Between two and five a Hindu child goes through a ceremony as it approaches the first stage. It is a family ceremony in the presence of a Hindu priest, when the Gayatri Mantra is chanted and a lock of hair cut.

The taking of the sacred thread by Brahmins occurs at about the age of seven. The cotton thread is placed over the boy's shoulders from left to right until he is married and becomes a householder, when it is placed from the right shoulder to the left by the guru or priest. Vows are taken accepting the physical, mental and spiritual duties of being a man. In a third stage of being, a Hindu must loosen his association with all social life, and in the fourth stage live the life of an ascetic.

Place of women in Hinduism

In Hinduism there is equality for women. They are much revered, and considered to have a very important role in the teaching of worship to the children.

Mandal

The *Mandal* is a *Swaminarayan* sect with its own scriptures, the *Vachnanrat* and the *Sikhshapatri*, which elaborate the ideology of *Moksha* (salvation). Mandal members believe in the Lord Swaminarayan as the supreme master of the universe, who endows his followers with the grace of salvation and liberates them from the cycle of death and rebirth. Their present-day spiritual leader, Swami Shri Muktajivandasji, is the bearer of divine grace and can grant *Moksha* to those who devote themselves to him.

Members call themselves *Kanbi Patels* and are divided into two groups; *Leva Kanbi Patels* and *Kadeva Kanbi Patels*. Within these groups all marriage and kinship relationships are formed.

A BRIEF TABLE OF COMPARISON BETWEEN HINDUISM AND CHRISTIANITY

HINDUISM

CHRISTIANITY
(The verses suggested here should not be used as 'proof text' but as pointers to the biblical doctrines.)

1 God

Many views of God:
  (*i*) polytheistic – belief in many gods
 (*ii*) monotheistic – belief in one god
(*iii*) monistic – belief in one impersonal force

One view of God: monotheistic. 'There is one God, and there is one who brings God and men together, the man Christ Jesus' (1 Timothy 2.5).

2 Trinity

There is Brahmā, the creator; Vishnu, the preserver; and Shiva, the destroyer and reproducer of

There is one God the Father, God the Son and God the Holy Spirit, forming one God and not three gods.
'Baptize them in the name of the Father

life. These are three
separate gods.

and of the Son and of the Holy Spirit'
(Matthew 28.19).
'You believed in Christ, and God put his
stamp of ownership on you by giving you
the Holy Spirit he had promised'
(Ephesians 1.13).

3 Incarnation

The god Vishnu came to
earth from time to time in
various incarnations. The
two most popular incar-
nations are Rama and
Krishna. The tenth incarnation, yet to come, is Vishnu
who will appear as the victorious Messiah.

'(God) condemned sin in human nature
by sending his own Son, who came with
a nature like a man's sinful nature to do
away with sin' (Romans 8.3).
'(Christ) has now appeared once and for
all' (Hebrews 9.6).

'Then the Son of Man will appear, coming in the clouds with great power and
glory' (Mark 13.26).

4 View of Man

Man has no separate identity from God. Thus man is
part of God, and God is part
of man.

Man and God are distinctively separate;
God is the creator and man the creation.
'For I am God and not man' (Hosea
11.9).

5 Salvation

(*i*) by works alone
(a) Karma mārga – the
way of action (sacrifice of
worship, ceremony)
(b) Jnana mārga – the way
of knowledge (meditation,
spiritual learning)
(c) Bhakti mārga – the way
of devotion

By faith in God, not works: 'For it is by
God's grace that you have been saved,
through faith. It is not your own doing,
but God's gift. There is nothing here to
boast of, since it is not the result of your
own efforts' (Ephesians 2.8–9).

(*ii*) all ways lead to God

only way to God is through Christ. 'Jesus
answered him: "I am the way, I am the
truth, I am the life; no one goes to the
Father except by me"' (John 14.6).
'Salvation is to be found through him
alone; for there is no one else in all the
world, whose name God has given to
men, by whom we can be saved' (Acts
4.12).

(*iii*) no definite founder

Jesus Christ the basis for our faith. 'Let
us keep our eyes fixed on Jesus, on whom
our faith depends from beginning to end'
(Hebrews 12.2).

6 Sin

No concept of original sin. Sin is regarded as ignorance of the oneness of Brahman.

Man is born sinful.

'Sin came into the world through one man, and his sin brought death with it. As a result, death spread to the whole human race, because all men sinned' (Romans 5.12).

7 After-life

Indefinite reincarnation unless the soul obtains release; then it is absorbed into the ultimate where it ceases to exist. There is no heaven or hell.

The believer goes to be with God in heaven.

'These then will be sent off to eternal punishment; the righteous will go to eternal life' (Matthew 25.46).

'Everyone must die once, and after that be judged by God' (Hebrews 9.27).

The Christian Approach to the Hindu

1 The Hindu believes that ultimately all ways lead to God, so it is wrong to preach that only one way is right. Because of this he will accept many fundamental truths of Christianity, such as the Trinity, and the incarnation of the Lord Jesus Christ, but will fit these truths into his Hindu system. Jesus is simply regarded as being another incarnation of Vishnu. One good method of approach is to take him to the New Testament where he can study the life and claims of the Lord Jesus. John's Gospel has the greatest appeal to the Hindu because of its spiritual depths and serene solemn spirituality. It is useful to ask a person to mark any points he wishes for discussion at the next visit.

2 When the message of the Gospel is presented to the Hindu, avoid using theological terms, which he will not understand. Biblical expressions convey a different meaning to him from the ones they convey to a Christian.

3 The Hindu is always drawn to a life of sacrifice, surrender and renunciation. Whereas the resurrection presents him with intellectual difficulties, he is naturally drawn to the cross both as a historical fact, and as a symbol of sacrifice and love. If the Hindu sees in the Christian a life of sacrifice, he will be far more ready to listen than to a thousand words of preaching.

4 Avoid arguments and being involved in philosophical speculation. Personal experience of God is invaluable, because the Hindu longs for peace with God, and to have experience of him.

5 Do not hesitate to pray with a Hindu. Prayer moves the atmosphere from the intellectual to the spiritual. Praying makes a good impression on the Hindu.

Three
Islam

If you were to ask a Muslim when Islam began, you would probably get an unexpected answer such as, 'It is as old as time; it is as old as God's creation; as old as Adam and Abraham and Moses; was not Abraham himself a Muslim, and his son Ishmael the father of the Arab race? Did not God establish his covenant with Ishmael for all generations? Did not Hagar find water for Ishmael at the well Zamzam in Mecca, which was one day to be the very heart of the Muslim world? Does not the Qur'an contain the unchangeable and eternal world of God, which was revealed in the Arabic tongue?' All this is part of the orthodox Muslim belief. If we are to find what is distinctive in the Muslim belief, we must first look at the person, character and career of the prophet Muhammad himself.

The prophet Muhammad

1 His background

Muhammad was born in the wealthy city of Mecca, which was a very important trading centre for Western Arabia, and on the main caravan routes. Mecca was also famous for its shrine the Ka'ba, and was the centre of pilgrimage for tribes throughout Arabia. Before Muhammad preached among them, the Arabs were mostly animists; some worshipped the stars and believed in spirits. However, at this time Muhammad came into contact with both Jews and Christians. The Jews, being traders, had settled in the trading cities on the caravan routes, taking with them their rabbis, scriptures and synagogues. Thus the Arabs had a superficial knowledge of the Old Testament stories and Jewish folklore, which we find in the pages of the Qur'an.

2 His early life

Muhammad was born about 570 AD of the tribe of Quraish. His father died before he was born, and his mother when he was six years old. His grandfather took care of him, but died shortly afterwards. He was then brought up by his uncle, Abu Talib. His contacts with Judaism and Christianity in Mecca influenced his later religious life.

A wealthy widow, Khadija, put him in charge of her caravans, and when he was 25 she rewarded his fidelity by marrying him. The marriage seems to have been surprisingly successful, for Muhammad took no second wife until after Khadija's death some twenty-five years later. A number of children were born to them, but only one daughter, Fatima, survived. Khadija's wealth enabled Muhammad to have a good deal of leisure time, and thus time for seclusion and prayer.

3 His later life and call
At the age of forty he began to experience visions which convinced him that God had a special task for him. One day when he was meditating in a cave on Mount Hira, outside the city of Mecca, he was visited by the angel Gabriel. The angel commanded him to preach God's warning to men.

4 The first converts
The response to his preaching was poor. His first converts included his nephew who was only nine years old at the time of his first revelation, and his adopted son who had formerly been his slave. The first adult to make profession of Islam was Abu Bakr, a wealthy merchant, who was a significant early convert. There were fifty converts during the period of 610–613 AD.

5 Opposition
Six years after the beginning of Muhammad's call and mission, there was such strong opposition to him that many of his followers had to flee from Mecca and found refuge in the Christian kingdom of Abyssinia. It was a long hard struggle for another six years. Then Muhammad took the decisive step of withdrawing with his followers, some two hundred in all, from Mecca to Medina. He had been invited there by a party of its inhabitants who had met him, accepted his claims and prepared their fellow townsmen for his advent. This withdrawal or *hijra* was the turning point in Muhammad's career, and has been chosen to mark the beginning of the Muslim era (622 AD). In Mecca he had been the rejected prophet pointing his countrymen to the one true God and warning them of judgment to come. In Medina he became at once the statesman, legislator and judge.

6 *Jewish opposition to Islam*

At first Muhammad recognized the validity of the Jewish and
Christian religions, being content to preach as the prophet to his
own people. Jerusalem was chosen as the direction in which man
should face when praying, and he adopted several Jewish practices. However, friction developed when the Jewish tribes failed to
recognize him as a true prophet or to practise the customs of
Islam.

Troubled by this, Muhammad began to assert the absolute
character of the revelation which had been given to him, and
claimed that it was a renewal of the religion that Abraham had
professed. In this way he gave up any attempt to reconcile Islam
with Judaism. It was towards the Ka'ba at Mecca that the Muslim
community were now to face during prayer and not towards
Jerusalem as previously commanded.

7 *The spread of Islam*

As Muhammad's power and influence increased so did large scale
warfare, conquering the whole of Arabia, and stamping on it the
religion of Islam. After he died in AD 632, aged 63 years, Islam
continued to spread until it became one of the dominant religions
of mankind. Muhammad was the first man to unify the Arabs into
one people. Muslims number about one seventh of the world
population, approximately 500 million.

The Qur'an – The Book of Islam

The Qur'an was revealed to Muhammad during the last 23 years
of his lifetime. The Muslim is a fundamentalist and the Qur'an
holds a place of exalted reverence in his heart. The Qur'an is said
to have existed eternally in heaven in its present form and
language – Arabic – so Arabic is the holy language that God
himself speaks. Speakers of Arabic have a special prestige in the
eyes of the Muslim world.

The content of the Qur'an

The Qur'an is about the same length as the New Testament, and
was said to have been delivered to Muhammad by the angel
Gabriel. The prophecies were not delivered in any systematic
order, and were thus subject to a great deal of rearrangement both
during Muhammad's own lifetime and after his death, when the
complete book was edited from scraps of parchment, tablets of

stone, camel's shoulder blades etc. The chapters as we have them are not arranged in any chronological order, and many contain prophecies or parts of prophecies which were preached at different times and refer to different circumstances. With the exception of the first sura, or chapter, which is a prayer addressed to God, it is God himself and not the prophet who is the speaker.

The Qur'an is divided into 114 chapters or suras, arranged roughly according to length. The first sura is a prayer which is used daily by the Muslim, and has a similar place in Islam to the Lord's Prayer in the life of a Christian. It is:

Praise be to God
The Lord of the worlds,
The merciful,
The compassionate,
The Lord of the Day of Judgment.
It is thee we serve,
And to thee we call for help.
Guide us in the straight path,
The path of those on whom thou has bestowed good,
Not of those on whom anger falls,
Or those who go astray.

The earliest suras bear some comparison to the psalms in length, subject matter and rhythmic form. They differ in approach, however, as they are not the striving of the human heart after God, but God speaking to man and using the prophet as a mouthpiece.

The significance of the Qur'an

Muhammad is seen as the last, but not the only prophet of God. Muslims do not worship any of the prophets but consider them examples and models for mankind. Thus Muslims dislike being called Muhammadans as they claim that they are not worshippers of Muhammad, but of Allah. None of the prophets was considered divine, but all were servants of God, and human. Muhammad was the final messenger, and the Qur'an the final message of God to mankind. The Qur'an plays a special part in the lives of most Muslims, who have to recite a section or verses from it five times per day in their prayers, and try to learn by heart as many verses as possible. No pious Muslim would ever drink, smoke, or make a noise while the Qur'an is being read aloud.

The Beliefs of Islam – the six articles of faith

1 *Allah*

The central point of Islam is the unity of God, and it is against any idea or concept which might tend to associate anything with God, either as equal or partner. Thus God is said to have no partner, or wife or children. He is one, a self-existent unity. Muslims deny the Trinity and the Lordship of the Lord Jesus Christ. This is because they interpret the sonship of Jesus literally and physically, and say that Christians believe that the Virgin Mary was the Mother of God. Jesus is depicted by the Qur'an as the great miracle worker and one of the greatest of the prophets. The Qur'an emphatically denies that he ever died on a cross; instead, when the Jews sought to crucify him, God called him up to heaven and threw his likeness on someone else who was crucified by mistake in his place. Traditions add that Christ is to come again, and have children, to break the symbol of the cross and acknowledge Islam.

The God of the Qur'an is the God of judgment and justice. God demands that human conduct shall be given its due reward or punishment.

Muslims believe that God created the heaven and the earth in six days. His work did not end with creating heaven and earth but his activities are still going on. The creation of Adam and Eve in heaven was the start of man. Adam and Eve were simultaneously deceived by Satan, who tempted them to eat the forbidden fruit. God accepted their repentance, the sin was forgiven, and both were sent down to earth. Muslims believe all children are born free from sin, and if they die during childhood they are sinless and go to live in paradise.

2 *Angels*

Great prominence is given to angels in the Qur'an, and anyone who denies them is an infidel. They are regarded as servants of God through whom he reveals his will. The greatest is Gabriel or Jibril, the revealer of God to Muhammad, who is also called the Holy Spirit. It is he who strengthened Jesus. The other archangels include Michael or Mika'il, Israfil, the trumpeter of doom, and 'Izra'il, the custodian and the one that has the care of the faithful at death. There are also an indefinite number of ordinary angels. Two recording angels attend on every man; one on his right records his good deeds, and the one on the left his sins. There are also two angels called Munkar and Nakir, who visit every newly buried corpse in the grave. Making the corpse sit up, these angels examine it in the faith. If the replies are satisfactory it is allowed to sleep in peace, but if it does not confess the apostle Muhammad they beat it severely, some say until the day of resurrection. Animals are said to hear its cries, although mortals cannot. The angels are fighting for believers against evil spirits. There are also demons or jinns.

3 The Scriptures

Jews, Christians and Muslims are regarded as people of the book. Muslims hold that the Law was revealed to Moses, the Psalms to David, the Gospel to Jesus, and the Qur'an to Muhammad. They claim that Jews and Christians have changed and distorted their own scriptures, so God sent the Qur'an as the final revelation to man.

4 The Prophets

Muslims accept all the prophets of the Old Testament, and John the Baptist in the New Testament. They believe that Jesus was the greatest of the prophets prior to Muhammad. He was the sinless one, not the son of God but the servant of God. Muhammad was the final prophet or warner. To disobey him leads to the fires of hell. Muhammad is not regarded as sinless, but as needing the forgiveness of God. The fact of Muhammad being a sinner is taken as a virtue, as he is able to sympathize with others.

5 The day of judgment

Muslims hold that the Judgment Day has been appointed by Allah, and will be preceded by gigantic natural catastrophes. On that day the righteous will be presented with a book of his deeds in his right hand, and the damned with the book in his left hand. It is only one's works that will be taken into account.

Everyone must walk on the *syrat* or path on the brink of hell, which is sharper than a sword's edge and finer than a hair. The righteous with his book in his right hand will walk across into heaven; the sinner will not be able to get across but will fall into the fires of hell. The righteous will thus enter paradise where all material gifts will be lavished upon him, and he will engage in physical pleasures.

6 The decrees of Allah

Everything is dependent on the will of Allah, and is preordained. This includes belief, disbelief and condemnation. There is a tendency to deny free will (though not all accept this tendency) so fatalism can result. As the Qur'an says: 'Allah wills what he wills.'

The five pillars of Islam – the practical duties

A Muslim is expected to practise the five pillars of Islam, which are the practical duties. These are:

1 Recital of kalima *or creed*
The creed is a simple one:

> 'There is no God but God, and Muhammad is the prophet of God.'

A recital of the creed is enough to enroll a new convert into the ranks of Islam.

2 Prayer
Ritual prayer plays a large part in the life of the devout Muslim. *Salat* is the name given to the prescribed worship with ritual movements which must be performed five times a day, at the fixed times. These prayers are compulsory for men and women over the age of ten, and may be performed alone, or in a congregation. There is more merit if they are offered in a mosque.

Before prayer a Muslim must clean himself, a ritual which is known as ablutions. This consists of repeating the name of Allah, the Beneficent, the Merciful, while he washes his face, arms, hands, ankles and feet with clean water.

(i) The call to prayer

Before the beginning of each set of daily prayers in the mosque, the muezzin goes up and calls the faithful to prayer, crying, 'God is the greatest, I bear witness that Muhammad is the messenger of Allah. Come to prayer. Come to security. God is the greatest.'

Once inside the mosque the congregation take up their positions facing Mecca. There are set postures to be adopted. Each of these is called a *raka*, and consists of eight separate acts of devotion. For the first three acts the Muslim stands, for the fourth he bows, for the fifth he stands, and for the sixth he kneels, his forehead touching the ground. He then kneels up, bows down to the ground again and then kneels again. Once the required number of *rakas* has been performed, the ceremony is completed by saying, 'Peace be upon you and the mercy of God'. The Muslim has to pray two *rakas* at dawn, four at midday, four in the afternoon, three just after sunset, and four *rakas* ninety minutes after sunset.

(ii) The Mosque

The Mosque is the focal point of the Muslim's devotions. It must have a court or fountain to provide pure water for ablutions. Other features include a pulpit, a lectern carrying a copy of the Qur'an, and a *mihrab*, which is a small recess shaped like a semi-circle facing in the direction of Mecca. All Muslims face the *mihrab* during prayers. Women are not prohibited from attending the services in the mosque, but are not encouraged to do so because of the responsibilities of the home. However, women often do attend services, and many mosques have special quarters for the women to worship in.

3 Fasting

Fasting means abstaining from food, drink, smoking and sexual intercourse from dawn to sunset, in the month of *Ramadan*. It is compulsory for all men, women and children above the age of ten, who are not sick, weak or old. It is primarily a spiritual and moral discipline, and man is thus taught to conquer his physical desires. Because the Muslim calendar is lunar, *Ramadan* falls at a different time each year.

4 Almsgiving

There are two types. *Zakat* means purification, and is the amount which a Muslim must give annually. It consists of one fortieth of money and merchandise, one tenth or one twentieth of agricultural produce, and different rates for cattle etc. *Zakat* is described as the wealth taken away from the rich and given to the poor. The second type is *sadaqah* or free will offering. This offering is regarded as a solemn duty, as generosity is highly regarded in Islam.

5 Hajj *or pilgrimage to Mecca*

This is obligatory to those who can afford it once in a lifetime. There is great merit in going to Mecca, to ask for forgiveness and to perform the ritual around the black stone or *Ka'ba*. Muslims believe that the casting out of Ishmael by Abraham was so that Ishmael could establish a shrine at Mecca. The sacrifice of a ram instead of Ishmael (not Isaac) underlies the pilgrimage.

Death

Muslims believe that the state after death is a complete representation of the state of life in its present form. The after-life will not be a new life but only an image and manifestation of this life.

On his death bed the Muslim (if capable) repeats the formula, 'There is no God if not God himself'. The body is bathed before the saying of funeral prayers and then taken to be buried. The grave is dug parallel to Mecca and the face is turned towards it. Some Muslims in Britain send the bodies home to be buried in large graveyards which are visited by pious men who pray for the dead in the life hereafter. This is the reason why certain Muslim communities in Britain ask for their own graveyards.

On death the soul receives a temporary body to taste the reward or punishment for his deeds in this life.

Prohibitions

The following things are prohibited for the Muslim: alcohol, eating the meat of animals not ritually killed, or strangled animals, pork, lending money on interest, gambling of all types, sex outside marriage, lying, stealing, cheating, murdering, and committing suicide. Animals to be eaten must be slaughtered in the name of God, otherwise the meat is forbidden.

Islamic Sects in Britain

Sunni and Shia

The great schism in the Islamic world is between the Sunni and Shia groups. The Sunni are the Orthodox muslims who believe that what is contained in the Qur'an and the *Sunna* define the limits of the beliefs and actions of Muslims. They regard the caliph (successor of Muhammad) as an ordinary man who has been nominated for his post as head of the community either by predecessor or popular vote.

The Shia began as a protest against the caliphate system of the Sunni. They believe that Muhammad left the guidance of the faithful in the hands of Ali, his cousin and son-in-law, therefore they say that the leadership of Islam should centre in Muhammad's family. The Shia believed in the doctrine of an infallible, divinely appointed, Imam in every age to whom God entrusted the guidance of his servants. This continued until the disappearance of the 12th (though some say 7th) Imam in 874 AD, who they say is now in hiding until the day of judgment. This belief in all Imams is exalted into an additional pillar of Islam. About 20% of all Muslims are Shi'ites, although the group has several subdivisions.

Ismailis

The Ismaili sect has approximately 20 million adherents, about 8,000 of whom have settled in Britain. It was mainly as students that they first came to Britain in any number. In 1957 a central *Jamatkhana* (mosque) was built in Kensington to serve all the Ismaili community, but the size of the community has multiplied so many times since then that halls and buildings have to be hired for meetings.

The Ismailis are a branch of the Shia sect and are the only group who accord to a living figure the status of Imam who is the inheritor of the spiritual and temporal mantle of the Prophet. The 49th Imam is Karim al-Huseyn, the present day Aga Khan. The Ismailis believe that they are indebted to the Imam and so tithe (*dassondh*) 10% of all they have for him, this money being collected at the monthly festival of Chandrat. Birthday gifts are also given to the Imam, the size of which is of competitive element within the community.

Ahmadiyya Movement

This most recent sect of Islam was founded by Mirza Ghulam Ahmad of India at the end of the last century. He himself claimed to be the promised Messiah whom God had appointed for reforming mankind and re-establishing the superiority of Islam over all other religions. The sect however has now formed two major groups, their main division occurring over the status of Ahmad. The first group, the Qadianis, say that Ahmad was a prophet, but the seceders say he was merely a reformer. In Britain the former group have a mosque in London and the latter have a mosque in Woking.

The distinctive doctrines of the Ahmaddiya are:
1 No verse of the Qur'an can be abrogated.
2 'Holy war' has lapsed and coercion in religion is condemned.
3 Muhammad was not the last prophet.
4 Jesus is dead and did not ascend bodily into heaven.
5 Hell is not everlasting.
6 Apostasy is not punishable by death.

7 Any innovation in religious practice is culpable.
8 Catholic consent is generally limited to the prophet's companions.
9 Revelation is the privilege of the true believer only.
10 Belief in Ahmad as Messiah Mahdi.
11 Spirituality in religion is more important then legalism.
12 The mediaeval ulama of the Qur'an need not be followed in interpretation.

3, 4 & 10 are anathema to orthodox Muslims and on more than one occasion numbers of Ahmadis have been massacred.

The Ahmadis claim that they seek to uplift humanity and establish peace throughout the world. They claim they are muslims 'real and true'. The orthodox Muslims however disagree with their doctrines and feel this sect should be declared a non-muslim minority.

A BRIEF TABLE OF COMPARISON BETWEEN ISLAM AND CHRISTIANITY

ISLAM

CHRISTIANITY

1 God
Unity of God. He has no equal partner or son.

Trinity of God the Father, God the Son and God the Holy Spirit. Not three gods but a unity of the Godhead. 'Baptize them in the name of the Father and of the Son and of the Holy Spirit' (Matthew 28.19).

2 Creation
God created the heaven and earth in six days. His work did not end with that act, but his creative act is still going on.

'And on the seventh day God finished his work which he had done, and he rested on the seventh day from all his work which he had done. So God blessed the seventh day and hallowed it, because on it God rested from all his work which he had done in creation' (Genesis 2.2–3).

3 Jesus Christ
(*i*) Not the son of God

The Son of God.
'A voice said from heaven. "This is my own dear Son, with whom I am well pleased"' (Matthew 3.17).

(*ii*) The virgin birth

(*iii*) Jesus was a great miracle worker, one of the greatest of the prophets.

Jesus the fulfilment of the law and the prophets.
'Do not think that I have come to do away with the Law of Moses and the teaching of the prophets. I have not come to do away with them, but to give them real meaning' (Matthew 5.17).

(*iv*) No crucifixion or resurrection.

'Jesus our Lord . . . was given over to die because of our sins and was raised to life to put us right with God' (Rom. 4.25).

4 The Second Coming

Christ is to come again and have children, to break the symbol of the cross and acknowledge Islam. There is a day of judgment appointed by God.

Christ is to come again to judge.
'Then the Son of Man will appear, coming in the clouds with great power and glory. He will send out the angels to the four corners of the earth and gather God's chosen people from one end of the world to the other' (Mark 13.26–27).

5 Sin

(*i*) Adam and Eve sinned simultaneously in heaven, both being deceived by Satan who tempted them to eat the forbidden fruit. God accepted their repentance, the sin was forgiven, and both sent down to earth.

Satan tempted Eve to sin, on earth. Eve then tempted Adam to sin.
'So when the woman saw that the tree was good for food, and that it was a delight to the eyes, and that the tree was to be desired to make one wise, she took of its fruit and ate; and she also gave some to her husband, and he ate' (Genesis 3.6).
'The Lord God sent him forth from the Garden of Eden, to till the ground from which he was taken' (Genesis 3.23).

(*ii*) Children are born sinless.

Man is born sinful.
'Sin came into the world through one man, and his sin brought death with it. As a result, death spread to the whole human race, because all men sinned' (Romans 5.12).

(*iii*) Jesus was sinless, Muhammad sinful.

'Christ was without sin, but God made him share our sin in order that we, in union with him, might share the righteousness of God' (2 Corinthians 5.21).

6 Salvation

Only works are taken into account.	Salvation is by faith not works.
	'It is by God's grace that you have been saved, through faith. It is not your own doing, but God's gift. There is nothing here to boast of, since it is not the result of your own efforts' (Ephesians 2.8–9).

7 Heaven

A place of sensuous pleasure where all material gifts will be lavished upon the righteous, and they will engage in physical pleasures.	A place of worship and holiness.
	'The twenty-four elders fall down before the one who sits on the throne, and worship him who lives for ever and ever. They throw their crowns before the throne, and say, "Our Lord and God! You are worthy to receive glory, and honour, and power"' (Revelation 4.10–11).

8 Prophets

Accepts all the prophets of the Old Testament, and John the Baptist and Jesus in the New Testament. Believe that Muhammad was the final prophet.	Accepts all the prophets, but Jesus is greater than all of them.
	'In the past God spoke to our ancestors many times and in many ways through the prophets, but in these last days he has spoken to us through his Son' (Hebrews 1.1).

9 Angels

(*i*) They are servants of God.	Messengers of God.
(*ii*) The greatest is Gabriel. He is called the Holy Spirit, and brought the message of God to Muhammad.	Gabriel is the angel who appeared to Daniel, Mary and Zacharias.

The Christian approach to Islam

One striking feature of Islam is that it does not separate the sacred side of life from the secular. Thus a man living in a Muslim community cannot fail to be affected by his religion even though he may have strong convictions of his own. For a man to elect out of Islam would be to cut himself off from his fellow men. Consequently it is easier to make an outward compliance (like attendance at the mosque) than to defy or ignore his religious obligations. We need to bear this in mind as we present the Gospel to Muslims.

Muhammad was influenced by Christianity and Judaism. Points of similarity provide a good basis for starting a discussion. Some ways of approach:

1 By starting at the prophets which the Muslim accepts, one can lead up to the coming of Christ. By dwelling on the person and claims of our Lord pray that the Holy Spirit might open his eyes to perceive the truth.

2 Islam is weak on teaching about sin. There is no true mediator between God and man for the Muslim. By discussing the righteousness of God from Romans, and thus showing the seriousness of sin in God's sight, one can lead on to the salvation offered in Christ, and communion with God through the work He has done.

3 The Muslim is a person with personal needs which Christ alone can meet. Understanding and sympathetic words can lead to personal testimony. The Christian should tell the Muslim how he came to know God, to be forgiven, to have peace with God, and how he has assurance that when he dies he will go to heaven. It is useful to give actual personal examples of how God has answered prayer.

4 Encourage the reading of the scriptures. Luke's Gospel is the most effective as it includes a genealogy which is acceptable to the Muslim. Encourage him to read about Christianity from Christian books with the aim of showing the scriptures are not corrupted.

5 Commend the high standard of Muslims.

6 If the authenticity of scripture is questioned ask for points which have been changed to be pointed out. Explain about the early manuscripts available before Muhammad. This subject can lead to profitable discussion and Bible study, as many Muslims will read scripture and answer questions.

Four
Sikhism

Who is a Sikh?

'A Sikh is a man or woman who believes in the One Immortal Being, the ten Gurus, the Ad Granth Sahib, and the word and teaching of all ten Gurus, the tenth Guru's baptism, and who does not believe in any other religion' (Official Book of Worship and Discipline issued by the Shromani Parbandhak Committee of Amritsar, dated 1950).

His Racial Origin

In the era 2000 BC the inhabitants of the great Asiatic steppelands became migrants, moving in three main directions. Those who travelled southeastwards entered Northern India, and this is known as the Aryan invasion. These tribes were musical, poetic, and great lovers of the family unit. From them the caste system evolved. The four main castes were:

 (*i*) *Brahman* or priestly caste
 (*ii*) *Vaisya* or merchant caste
 (*iii*) *Kshatriya* or warrior caste
 (*iv*) *Sudra* or labouring caste

Two of the branches of the *Kshatriya* caste were the *Rajputs* (traders) and the *Jats* (those wedded to the soil). From these castes came the founders and the bulk of the early adherents of the Sikh religion. The founders were called gurus.

The Location of the Sikh today

The Sikh originates in the region of the Punjab a largely rural environment in Northern India. The 1971 Census of India gave the number of Sikhs as just under eleven million. The 1947 partition of India forced hundreds of thousands of Sikhs to leave their rich lands and migrate eastwards. However their mechanical skills and enterprise have made them welcome in a number of countries. There are now large colonies of Sikhs to be found in Singapore,

Hong Kong, British Columbia, East Africa, Iran, the United States, Fiji and Great Britain.

The beginnings and development of Sikhism

The founder of the Sikh religion was Guru Nanak, who was born in 1469 in Talwandi, which is near Lahore in Pakistan. He came from a high caste Hindu family, and received a good education. However, in his early life he rejected the Hindu beliefs. As he grew older he loved God's name and creation more and more, and thought that religion should be simple enough for all men to understand and practise. He believed that everyone should have direct communication with God, and that no one should have special privileges by reason of birth, wealth, religion, race and sex. People should regard themselves as equal under the fatherhood of God. He taught that the way of salvation was by leading a good honest life of kindness and generosity towards others, a life of activity and endeavour within the society and family. He was very missionary-minded, travelling extensively with his message. He died in 1539, aged 70, and was loved by Hindus and Muslims alike.

The Guruship

1 Guru Nanak (1469-1539): Founded Sikhism
2 Guru Angard (1504-1552): Introduced the *Gurmukhi* script.
3 Guru Amar Das (1479-1574): Advance in organising Sikhs as a community.
4 Guru Ram Das (1534-1581): Founded the holy city – Amritsar.
5 Guru Arjan (1563-1606): Compiled the *Ad Granth*, and built the Golden Temple at Amritsar.
6 Guru Harogovind (1595-1644): Started the military organization of the Sikhs to fight against religious persecution.
7 Guru Har Rai (1630-1661): Consolidated the organization of the Sikhs on peaceful lines.
8 Guru Harkishan (1656-1664): Appointed at the age of five, he healed the sick.
9 Guru Teg Bahadur (1621-1675): Founder of many *Gurdwaras* (Sikh temples).
10 Guru Gobind Singh (1666-1708): Established the *Khalsa*. Completed the Ad Granth. Ended the line of Gurus and ordained the *Ad Granth* as the future guide of the Sikhs.

The tenth guru, Gobind Singh, believed that through the teachings and writings of the ten gurus sufficient stress had been placed on the moral and spiritual aspects of the faith, and that it was therefore unnecessary to perpetuate the cult of human leadership in the form of the gurus. He determined to end the line of gurus, giving the Sikhs a form of organization on more democratic lines. In 1699 he introduced a form of initiation for the Sikhs, and enjoined the initiates to follow certain principles and to wear a uniform. At a certain Spring festival (at a time when Muslims seemed determined to exterminate the followers of Sikhism) the guru demanded the head of someone who was prepared to die for the cause of Sikhism. Five men offered their lives. Instead of chopping off their heads, he declared them true Sikhs, and gave them the responsibility of forming the core of the new brotherhood, from that time termed *Khalsa*. This took on the force of a military body.

He initiated the five by sprinkling a holy sweetened water over their heads, and established the five symbols which all initiated Sikhs should wear. He also declared that men should adopt the name *Singh*, and women the name *Kaur*.

The Five Symbols

(*i*) Keshas − uncut hair
(*ii*) Kangha − the comb
(*iii*) Kara − the steel bangle
(*iv*) Kirpan − the short sword
(*v*) Kachh − pair of shorts as underwear

The members of the brotherhood comprise the *Khalsa*. All members of the *Khalsa* should wear the above symbols. These symbols have both a practical and a deep spiritual meaning to the Sikh. The long hair is a symbol of holiness, and is associated in India with saintliness. It indicates moral and spiritual strength. The turban has become an essential accompaniment to the unshorn hair. In Britain the Sikh has had difficulties when employers have demanded that he wear a uniform headgear in place of a turban. In Britain the law forbids the carrying of a sword so a pin is usually worn.

The two main ceremonies of Sikhism

1 Amrit or initiation
Any man or woman, of whatever nationality, race or social stan-

ding, who is prepared to accept the rules governing the Sikh community has the right to receive initiation. There is no minimum age but those receiving it should have reached maturity. Some people compare the significance of this initiation ceremony to that of confirmation.

During the long ceremony promises are made, many prayers are said and many rules read. Recitation of prayers takes place around a bowl of nectar being stirred with a sword. Following this the initiated become true members of the *Khalsa* and wear the symbols.

2 Marriage

This ceremony is held in high esteem. It is largely a religious ceremony, and is considered the union of two souls: a Sikh must marry a Sikh. There is much hymn singing, reading and praying during the ceremony. The most important part is when the bride and groom walk round the Ad Granth four times while four verses of the marriage hymn are sung.

The Holy Book

The Sikh Holy Book is called *Ad Granth* or *Guru Granth Sahib* or *Adi Granth.* It comprises devotional readings, exhortation, instruction, and religious dialogues. There is no historical narrative or prose teaching. In general the poetry is reminiscent of Psalms and Proverbs.

The beliefs of the Sikh

'There is One God,
His name is truth,
The All-pervading Creator,
Without fear, without hatred,
Immortal, Unborn, Self-existent,
By grace, the Enlightener.
True in the beginning, True throughout the ages,
True even now, Nanak, and forever shall be True.'

Every Sikh knows this verse from the *Ad Granth* as it forms the basis of his religious belief.
The main beliefs are:

1 Monotheism. Belief in one God, the supreme divine spirit, who is the origin and destination of all souls. The same God is worshipped under different names by all mankind. He is the God of Hindu, Sikh, Jew, Muslim and Christian at the same time.

2 The ultimate way of obtaining salvation is by meditation on the name of the divine spirit, by recitation.

3 Truthful living and service to mankind, according to the guru's teaching.

4 Study of the scriptures.

5 Reincarnation. Man's soul, being part of the eternal soul, has existed from the time of the creation, and until the time it is reabsorbed it remains separate and is subject to death and rebirth.

6 Life is not sinful in its origin.

Death

For the Sikh, death is the gateway through which the believer must pass to enjoy the bliss of God's presence. Because of this there is no noisy wailing or outward expression of mourning. The body is washed and dressed complete with all five symbols of Sikhism before a simple service at the crematorium. Hymns are sung and the *Sohila*, or bedtime prayer, is recited as the body is commended to God. After the cremation the relatives will read the *Ad Granth* from beginning to end. When this is done the 'mourning' period will end with a final service.

Sikhs like Hindus believe in transmigration, but hold that liberation comes only by the grace of God, the supreme Guru who has revealed himself through the ten gurus.

The practical outworking of the Sikh beliefs

This is of utmost importance. Sikhism is living the life. A Sikh's life should show:

No offence to other faiths; hospitality; worship of one God, i.e. no idol worship; no dealings with caste, black magic, or superstitious practices; no ancestor worship, no star or moon reading; *Gurdwara* (temple) to serve as centre of worship;

Teaching of Sikhism to the children;

Wearing of long hair;

Boys have the name *Singh*, and girls the name *Kaur*;

There should be no alcohol drinking, tobacco or drug taking;

Condemnation of infanticide;

Honest working;

No adultery;

Respect of women: all are equal.

Sikh worship

A Sikh may worship:

1 In the home. Many have a room set aside for the Holy Book, the *Ad Granth*.

2 In the temple which is called a *gurdwara*. One large room which contains the *Ad Granth* is used for prayer and worship. Before entering the worshipper must remove his shoes and cover his head. He then approaches the Holy Book, and bowing to the floor, he places an offering, usually of money, on the edge of the covering cloth. He then backs away keeping his face respectfully towards the *Ad Granth* and sits on the floor.

Anyone may conduct the prayers or perform the ceremonies, and in this respect men and women are absolutely equal. Services begin with the singing of hymns accompanied by drums, harmonies etc.

The hymns are interspersed with lectures, poems or stories from Sikh history, always ending with the *Ardas*, a prayer invoking God's grace on the Sikhs. A final verse is read from the Holy Book, and then a type of sweet semolina pudding is distributed. During the prayer the sacred food is blessed and a sword run through it symbolically to strengthen the *Khalsa* or Brotherhood.

The *gurdwara* is also the guest house for passing travellers. At festivals the whole congregation feasts there. *Gurdwaras* are generally managed by committees, properly elected by the congregation. There is no priesthood, but a *Granthi* is usually employed to take care of the buildings and conduct the prayers.

A BRIEF TABLE OF COMPARISON BETWEEN SIKHISM AND CHRISTIANITY

SIKHISM	CHRISTIANITY
1 God He is one. His name is truth. He is omnipotent and merciful.	
2 Salvation (*i*) All ways lead to God. God is the God of the Hindu, Muslim, Jew, Sikh and Christian at the same time.	Jesus Christ is the only way. 'Jesus answered him: "I am the way, I am the truth, I am the life; no one goes to the Father except by me"' (John 14.6). 'Salvation is to be found through him alone; for there is no one else in all the

world, whose name God has given to men, by whom we can be saved' (Acts 4.12).

(*ii*) By works and grace, but mainly by works. All blessings come to us not through our own merit but by the grace of God, and at the same time our works in this life determine our next life.

By grace alone.
'For it is by God's grace that you have been saved, through faith. It is not your own doing, but God's gift. There is nothing here to boast of, since it is not the result of your own efforts' (Ephesians 2.8–9).

(*iii*) Reincarnation. It is necessary to have a long chain of rebirths to cast out sin.

Only one life on earth.
'Everyone must die once, and after that be judged by God' (Hebrews 9.27).

(*iv*) Only the Guru (God) can cut short this chain and grant deliverance.

Christ alone can give salvation.
See *(i)*.

3 Sin

Man is basically good, but has become impure through contamination from outside.

Man is born sinful.
'Sin came into the world through one man, and his sin brought death with it. As a result, death spread to the whole human race, because all men sinned' (Romans 5.12).

4 Incarnation

God is unborn.

God became man in Jesus Christ. 'He became like man, he appeared in human likeness' (Philippians 2. 7).
'The Word became a human being and lived among us' (John 1. 14).

5 Holy Spirit

The Sikh could be said to take on the spirit of the Guru. This is however through self effort. The Sikh way of life offers an ideal, but not the power to attain it.

The Christian has power within him in the form of the Holy Spirit.
'Keep the good things that have been entrusted to you, through the power of the Holy Spirit who lives in us' (2 Timothy 1.14).
'Let the Spirit direct your lives, and do not satisfy the desires of the human nature' (Galatians 5.16).

6 After-life

Future lives depend on deeds done in this one.

Believers go to be with God.
'These, then, will be sent off to eternal

punishment; the righteous will go to eternal life' (Matthew 25.46).

7 Holy Scriptures

Sikhs follow closely the writings of the Gurus. They are 'People of the Book'. By following the writings of the Gurus, they can obtain spiritual heights.

Christians believe the Bible is inspired by God.

'All Scripture is inspired by God and is useful for teaching the truth, rebuking error, correcting faults, and giving instruction for right living, so that the man who serves God may be fully qualified and equipped to do every kind of good work' (2 Timothy 3.16–17).

The Christian approach to the Sikh

On observing a Sikh's life of good works, his patience, hospitality, care for his fellow men, and his emphasis on grace and love, one might be led to think 'Ah! Here is a Christian'. In conversation one would learn otherwise, and realize that a knowledge of Jesus Christ as Saviour was lacking. How then, can we reach these kind-hearted people with the Gospel?

1 Sikhs love fellowship, having frequent gatherings in their *gurdwaras*, where all classes, colours and creeds are equally welcome. Friendship with the Sikhs is the first step. They know much of brotherhood, love and devotion. The use of a home is ideal, the Sikhs being great family lovers. A bond of friendship earns the right to speak about Jesus Christ.

2 One can align oneself with a Sikh by speaking of doing good to all mankind. This can lead to the example of Jesus Christ himself, the one who went so far as to die on the cross as a supreme sacrifice. The Sikh does not find the cross a barrier as an example of service to mankind, but that Jesus took our place as sin-bearer is problematic to him. From the crucifixion it is possible to lead on to the resurrection and speak of the power available in order to lead a godly life. Although the Sikh religion points to the ideal, they do not have the power to fulfil it.

3 The Gurus' lives are recorded in the Sikh literature. The life of Jesus is recorded in the Gospels. Encourage the reading of the life of Jesus Christ through the scriptures. Many of their writings are poetic, being similar in style to Psalms and Proverbs.

4 The Sikh believes that God is the God of all religions, therefore it is bad policy to begin by attempting to show that God is only in true communion with Christians. This point is better left until his confidence is truly won.

Five
Buddhism

'I go for refuge to the Buddha.
I go for refuge to the Dhamma (teaching).
I go for refuge to the Sangha (monks).'

With these words the devout Buddhist begins his meditation before an image of the Buddha. To understand Buddhism let us first look at the life of Buddha.

Life of the Buddha

According to Buddhist teachings, Buddha was born in 560 BC, as the son of a Rajah in the foothills of the Himalayas, on the south side of what is now Nepal. His family or clan name was Gautama and his personal name Siddhatta. It is held that this was the last of five hundred reincarnations during which he suffered, sacrificed, fulfilled every perfection and drew nearer to his goal of winning enlightenment for himself and all mankind. His family were Hindu by religion. At the age of sixteen he won his wife Yasodhara in a contest of arms and she bore him a son Ratula.

Despite all his father's efforts to keep the knowledge of wordly woes from his eyes, the young prince driving out from the palace saw an old man, then a sick man, then a dead man. When he enquired the meaning of these sights, he was told that this was what became of all men. He returned to the palace pondering deeply. On another drive from the palace he saw an ascetic with shaven head and yellow robe, and was told that this was one who had gone out to live the homeless life. During the night he felt the positive call to save not only himself but all mankind from birth into the world of suffering. He left his wife and child, and with his chariot and horse came to the edge of the forest, where he exchanged his princely robes with those of a beggar, and went out into the homeless life, alone.

His search for enlightenment

He was 29 years old when this began, but it was not rewarded until six years later. To begin with he put himself under the instruction of two Brahman hermits, but he was unable to find satisfaction in their teaching, for they could not tell him how to put an end to rebirth. He then joined with five companions in a life of extreme asceticism, existing, it is said, on a mere grain of rice each day, until his body was reduced almost to a skeleton. He still did not find enlightenment. He then turned away from such extremes. The ascetics with him left in disgust. Eventually as the culmination of prolonged meditation, he sat beneath the Bo (Wisdom) tree at Uruvela, and there received the thoughts which constitute the essential message of Buddhism. He had achieved enlightenment. It was the night of the full moon in May, and he was 35 years old. From this point on he was known as the Buddha – the One who knows.

Enlightenment achieved

This experience of reality within himself gave the Buddha supreme joy and peace. There and then he attained Nirvana (see later reference). Then Mara the evil one tempted him, and tried to persuade him to enter the fulness of Nirvana and not worry about the fate of mankind. Earth trembled as it waited for his reply, and Brahma (creator of the universe) pleaded with him for mankind. Mara was defeated, and so Buddha stayed in the world to share with men the way of escape from suffering.

Shortly afterwards he preached his first sermon, and soon gathered around himself a band of disciples. At the age of 80 he died. Just before his death he gave the *Dhamma* or teaching to his disciples.

The four noble truths

Buddhists would probably claim that words are inadequate to describe Gautama's enlightenment, but as far as they do it consists in following the four noble truths which are as follows:

1 The truth of suffering. This simply asserts that suffering is found everywhere, and all forms of existence are subject to it. It is closely bound up with individual existence.

2 The cause of suffering, which Gautama felt to be desire: desire for possession and selfish enjoyment of every kind, but particularly the desire for separate individual existence. Because of this desire man is attached to the wheel of reincarnation.

3 Suffering ceases when desire ceases, when this selfish craving, this lust for life, has been renounced and destroyed. When one's desire ceases this ceases the wheel of reincarnation and one can enter Nirvana.

4 The truth of the path which leads to the cessation of suffering. Gautama took over from Hinduism the doctrine of rebirth or reincarnation, teaching that people pass away and are reborn, according to their behaviour in a previous lifetime. He believed that only by detachment could a man's thoughts, words and actions be deprived of their power to bind him to the wheel of reincarnation. This path to detachment is also known as the middle way, avoiding the two extremes of self-indulgence and self-mortification, both of which Gautama had tested and found wanting.

The holy eight-fold path

The eight steps in this path are as follows:

1 Right views
This involves acceptance of the four truths, and a total rejection of all unworthy attitudes and acts.

2 Right desires
The thoughts are to be free from lust, ill-will and cruelty.

3 Right speech
This must be plain and truthful. Lying, tale-telling, harsh and vain talk is not acceptable.

4 Right conduct
This includes charity, and abstention from killing any living being. Even the breaking of an egg, which is potential life, is condemned. There must be no stealing, or unlawful sexual intercourse. In Buddhism morality and intellectual enlightenment are inseparable.

5 Right mode of livelihood
This must be without harming anyone and free from luxury. Each person must take up work which will give scope to his abilities and make him useful to his fellow-men.

6 Right effort
The climax of this achievement is universal love.

7 Right awareness

8 Meditation

This amounts to singlemindedness of thought, concentrating the mind on a single object, all hindrances having been overcome. Such mind development is the principal occupation of the more enlightened Buddhist, and an important part of the daily life of the humblest follower of Gautama. It leads into trances where the devotee is purified from all distractions and evils, and filled with rapture and happiness.

Buddhist Scriptures

1 *Theravada* Scriptures

Buddhist teachings have been handed down orally for centuries and were first written down in the first century BC in the Pali Canon, known as the *Tripitaka* ('Three Baskets') because it consisted of three separate collections of texts. These are:

a) *Vinaya-Pitaka* (the Discipline Basket) containing the monastic rules.

b) *Sutta-Pitaka* (the Discourse Basket) containing the collected discourse, songs and sayings of the Buddha.

c) *Abidhamma-Pitaka* (the Metaphysical Basket) containing the writings of later scholars on doctrines and ethics.

The *sutta-pitaka* contains the most popular and widely read texts including the *Dhammapadda* or 'Way of Virtue' which is probably the best known of all Buddhist sacred texts.

2 *Mahayana* Scriptures

The *Mahayana* scriptures were written in Sanskrit between AD 100 and 800 and are divided into three chief categories:

a) *Vinaya* which were the rules for religious orders.

b) *Sutras* which were the discourses (similar to the *Sutta-Pitaka*)

c) *Shastras* which were the philosophical discussions.

Mahayana scriptures have multiplied to the point that standard editions encompass over 5,000 volumes. Because of this great number most sects have chosen 'favourites' which they refer to exclusively.

Explanation of three Buddhist terms

1 *Arahant*ship

The steps of the eightfold path lead to *arahant*ship. This is the state of him who 'is worthy of him' who has reached the end of the eightfold path. The *arahant* is the Buddha saint. He has reached fulfilment. His energies are now purely spiritual; he no longer feels suffering and takes no pleasure in earthly joys. He is able to say 'I do not wish for death, I do not wish for life'. He waits in this state of calm contentment for the entrance into *nirvana* at death.

2 Nirvana

This seems a completely negative concept. It means the end, the blowing out of existence, so there is no more reincarnation.

3 Karma

This denotes the law of cause and effect, a law of moral compensation. A man's happiness or misery is the result of past deeds. As a man sows so shall he also reap.

An assessment of Buddhism

It can be seen from this statement of Buddhist doctrine that there is no mention of God. Gautama himself made no claim to divinity. He only professed to point out the way and to give guidance to those who try to walk in it. Gautama was only the teacher. God in the objective personal sense does not fit into the picture.

Buddhism as taught by its founder is in no sense a system of faith and worship. There is neither prayer nor praise. Gautama offered neither redemption or forgiveness or heaven. He did not warn of judgment or hell. Buddhism does not accept the view that by nature man is evil, nor does it seek any external agency for the carrying out of its moral precepts. It is addressed primarily to the problem of pain and suffering. Thus Buddhism is hardly a religion in the generally accepted sense of the word, as making contact between man and his maker. It is rather a moral philosophy and a way.

The Buddhist order

Gautama founded not a church but an order. The focal point of Buddhist life is the monastery. It is not for the many but for the few who are able to do it. They must have their heads shaven and wear a saffron robe.

Sanctions of the order

The first four are the great prohibitions:

1 Violence
2 Marriage
3 Stealing
4 Spiritual pride

The other sanctions are the renunciations. These are:

5 Alcohol
6 Over-eating
7 Dancing
8 Worldly entertainment
9 Perfume
10 High chair, seat or bed
11 Money

The monks spend their lives in meditation and study.

Mahayana Buddhism

Between the third century BC and the first century AD the doctrines of the Mahayana, the most elaborately developed form of Buddhism, began to take shape. This was a new development which effectively made Buddhism a world religion. Mahayana Buddhism arose because of the inability of Hinayana or orthodox Buddhism to cater for the religious needs of men.

Here are some of the most striking changes:

1 The introduction of a supreme reality by means of which the universe came into being.

2 Gautama is considered to be divine, a manifestation of this reality.

3 The development of *Bodhisattvas*. These are beings that have acquired inexhaustible stores of merit, and could readily achieve the full status of Buddhas and pass into *nirvana*. However, out of love and pity for suffering humanity, they have postponed their entrance into *nirvana*, and transfer their merit as the need arises to those who call upon them in prayer and devotion. They sit enthroned in the heavens, looking down on a needy world, and sometimes in redemptive pity descend in the guise of ministering angels to perform deeds of mercy.

4 The way of salvation is by faith in Gautama and the Bodhisattvas.

5 There are vivid portrayals of heaven and hell, and the hope of individual immortality is set before the follower.

6 Images were introduced to aid the illiterate, and idolatrous polytheism supplanted Gautama's original atheism.

Zen Buddhism

The Zen or meditative sect of Mahayana gets its name from the stress it lays on contemplation and meditation as opposed to study and all acquired knowledge. It teaches that enlightenment may be attained in this life by a sudden comprehension of our true natures.

Man and nature are not in opposition since man is part of nature or part of the Buddha. In Zen Buddhism beautiful things are contemplated, for example cherry blossom. This is done with such meditation that the object is said to absorb and possess the perceiver.

A highly disciplined technique of meditation has been worked out. This is termed *Zazen*, and calls for stated periods of meditation in a hall designed for the purpose. In Zen the familiar props of images and scriptures are excluded.

Death

Death is an incident in life of no more importance and finality than sleep. It is the gateway to a different form of life, and is usually looked upon as a well-earned rest. It is believed that the body dies at birth but the Karma lives on. The body is just a temporary garment so to mourn would be foolishness to the Buddhist.

The Buddha taught that each man suffers in the after-life the heaven or hell which he is manufacturing every hour of his life on earth. The 'day of judgment is at all times and for everyone ... today.'

A BRIEF TABLE OF COMPARISON BETWEEN HINAYANA BUDDHISM AND CHRISTIANITY

BUDDHISM	CHRISTIANITY
1 God	
No mention of God. Gautama made no claims of divinity, he only pointed out the way. Therefore Buddhism is a way of life and not a searching for God.	Personal yet transcendental God. *(i)* Personal as he came in the form of Jesus Christ. 'The Word became a human being and lived among us' (John 1.14).

(ii) Transcendent.

'Thine, O Lord, is the greatness, and the power, and the glory, and the victory, and the majesty;' (1 Chronicles 29.11).

2 Sin

(i) Gautama offered no forgiveness of sin

There is forgiveness of sin in Jesus Christ.

'Here is the Lamb of God who takes away the sin of the world' (John 1.29).

(ii) Man is not by nature evil

Man is born evil.

'Sin came into the world through one man and his sin brought death with it. As a result, death spread to the whole human race, because all men sinned' (Romans 5.12).

3 After-life

(i) No heaven, hell or judgment. The Buddhist saint enters Nirvana (extinction) at death.

Heaven for the believer, hell for the unbeliever.

'These, then, will be sent off to eternal punishment; the righteous will go to eternal life' (Matthew 25.46).

(ii) One who has not attained the end of the eight-fold path is reincarnated.

No reincarnation.

'Everyone must die once, and after that be judged by God' (Hebrews 9.27).

4 Salvation

The Buddhist is cast back on himself for salvation, to attain the lofty moral and social precepts with no external agency.

Salvation is through Jesus Christ.

'God loved the world so much, that he gave his only Son, so that everyone who believes in him may not die but have eternal life' (John 3.16).

The Holy Spirit gives inner strength, comforts and teaches.

'The Helper, the Holy Spirit, whom the Father will send in my name, will teach you everything, and make you remember all that I have told you' (John 14.26).

5 Main emphasis

On high moral and social standards – to attain the end of the Holy Eight-Fold path.

On faith in Jesus Christ.

'Let us keep our eyes fixed on Jesus, on whom our faith depends from beginning to end' (Hebrews 12.2).

Later developments
As Buddhism developed and
spread, there arose the belief
in salvation gods, and in
heaven, and Buddha himself
became divine, taking on
the form of a god.

The Christian approach to the Buddhist

1 The Buddhist tries to attain lofty moral and social standards by
his own unaided efforts. Christians can stress that salvation is not
by striving to attain such precepts but by faith in Jesus Christ.
Once we have accepted Christ we then have the strength and
power of the Holy Spirit to enable us to live a moral and pure life.

2 The Buddhist is drawn to a life of sacrifice, surrender and
renunciation. If the Buddhist sees a life of self-sacrifice in the
Christian he will be drawn to it. He will also be drawn to the
sacrifice of Jesus, and here it is possible to show the meaning of
the sacrificial life and death of Jesus.

3 The Buddhist has a great reverence for life. He does not believe
in taking any form of life. Christians need to point out that we
also believe in reverence for life – God cares and is concerned even
for the sparrows.

4 Buddhists regard life as an evil to be avoided as soon as possible. However, Christians regard life as a privilege entrusted to us
by God, to be lived and enjoyed. So we can show that a
Christ-centred life takes on a new fulfilment and purpose.

Six
Principal Festivals

Islam

The two principal feasts which have great religious and social importance in the life of a Muslim are the Breaking of the Fast at the end of the month of Ramadan, and the Sacrifice of the Pilgrimage. They are named the *Id-ul-Fitr* and the *Id-ul-Adha* respectively.

The *Id-ul-Fitr* is held on the first day of the month of *Shawal* and marks the end of the long month of fasting. It is a day of great rejoicing, on which the Muslim attends the mosque, gives alms and then enjoys a great feast.

The *Id-ul-Adha* is held on the tenth day of the month of *Dhul-Hijja* marking the end of the ceremonies of the pilgrimage of Ibrahim and the sacrifice of Ishmael. This is celebrated to remind the Muslim that one should not hesitate to sacrifice anything for the glory of God. Instead of giving alms, the sacrifice of an animal is obligatory.

Another festival is called *Muharram*. It commemorates the battle and death of Hussain, the grandson of the prophet. Muslims are directed to fast on this day.

There are a number of other festivals such as the Prophet Mohammed's birthday (*Id-milad-un-Nabi*).

All Muslim festivals are subject to the phases of the moon, and have to take into account the 'sighting' of the new moon. Often in Britain this is not possible because of low cloud, therefore Muslim religious leaders contact religious institutions based on Muslim countries where the new moon would have been sighted. The Hijri lunar year is 10–11 days shorter than the solar year (354–355). 71 days after the first of the month of Muharram (the first new year day) is the Prophet's Day. After 166 days is the fasting month of Ramadan (29–30 days), at the end of which is the Id-ul-Fitr. 264 days after the Prophet's Day is the Id-ul-Adha.

Sikhism

On January 18 is the Sikh celebration of Guru Gobind Singh's birthday. April 13 is *Baisakhi*, the first day of both the Sikh and Hindu new year. This commemorates the founding of the Khalsa, the society of the pure. For Sikhs this has special significance. Guru Amar Das, the third guru, made it one of the annual gatherings of the Sikhs, the other being *Diwali*. This enabled the Sikhs to have their own celebrations at a time when the Sikh religion was very much in its infancy.

The end of November to the beginning of December is the birthday of Guru Nanak, the founder of the Sikh faith, and the first of the ten gurus.

Hinduism

About March is the Hindu festival called *Holi*. Symbolically it represents the Indian harvest thanksgiving. According to the orthodox Hindu calendar, Krishna returns on this day to Gokul, the temple city of Brindaban 80 miles south of Delhi, playing his flute and dancing with the Gopis or milkmaids.

April 13 is *Baisakhi*, the first day of the Hindu new year. This is also named Martyr's Day.

About the end of August is *Janmashtami*, the nativity festival of Krishna. His birthplace was the prison of a tyrant, and legend has it that he was rescued from prison by the swapping of babies.

In October is *Dassehra*, again one of the unfixed dates depending on the full moon. This is one of the great Hindu festivals.

The beginning of November is *Diwali*, the Hindu festival representing the victory of the forces of good over evil. On this night the goddess *Lakshmi*, personification of good fortune and prosperity, visits homes lit with many lamps. The lamps are usually saucer-shaped earthenware *deepas* filled with coconut oil and rolled down cotton wicks.

Buddhism

There are three main festivals which the Buddhists celebrate: The Vesak Festival celebrates Buddha's birth, enlightenment and death. It is held that all these events took place at the same time of year, and they are now celebrated in May, depending on the lunar calendar.

The celebrations of Magha-Puja are held in February or March. They celebrate the event when Buddha delivered his discourse on the main principles of his teaching to about 1,250 disciples, who had gathered together without previous announcement. Buddha ordained them, and they were all liberated.

Asalha-Puja is the day on which Buddha preached his first discourse to the five ascetics. It is celebrated in July.

Seven
Points for consideration at church level

1 The Biblical teaching on the unity of mankind.

2 The social implications of the Gospel, for example the Christian's responsibility to demonstrate love and compassion practically.

3 The background, culture and religions of the immigrants.

4 The difficulties confronting them and the hostile treatment they receive at the hands of non-Christians.

5 The social tensions already existing within a parish which may lead to a worsening of relations between residents and new-comers.

6 The problems of race, immigration and integration on the national level, and of the true facts and statistics concerned.

7 How to overcome prejudice at the cross.

8 The use of homes which are the most effective base. They can be used especially for women and children. Children can frequently break down barriers.

Suggestions for meetings to be held at the church

1 An international evening when different races can be invited to a social gathering with church members.

2 A dialogue can be held between Christians and leaders of another religion e.g. Sikh leaders. This is a good method of presenting the Gospel.

3 Over lunch tensions, difficulties etc. can be discussed between leaders of the various communities in the town. Police representatives can also be invited.

4 Separate meetings for Asian Christians may be necessary because of language and cultural differences.
All these meetings need good organization and special preparation.

Practical hints when undertaking visitation

1 Attitudes

Our attitudes to the immigrant are very important. If they betray
a hint of coolness, of prejudice, of superiority or patronage, then
our work is nullified. Thus we need to be clear before God that we
are totally right with him and with other men before we start out.
The most important point to remember is that of friendliness. We
should always be open, friendly and kind. We must beware of
reserve, as it can be interpreted as expressing superiority.
Remember that we are ambassadors for Christ. We represent him,
thus we are to be motivated by his love and are to demonstrate
his compassion.

2 Consideration of culture

In preparation we need to consider the method of approach which
would be most suitable to the particular religion and culture of
those we intend to visit. Remember that the Indian and Pakistani
have established cultures of their own, cultures that have existed
for many hundreds of years. Thus we must note their attitude to
the place of men and women, to dress, children, hospitality etc. It
is essential to know these things as it would be easy to give the
wrong impression or make unnecessary mistakes.

3 Personnel

Married couples are the ideal team units. But in Asian culture it is
improper for unmarried mixed couples to be seen in public, so if
married couples are not available, pairs of workers of the same sex
should be used. It is regarded as improper even to talk to a
member of the opposite sex, so avoid this too if at all possible.

4 Dress

Dress to the Asian is important. One should be neat and tidy and
preferably conservative in taste. Modesty in women is essential,
for example the Asian regards the mini-skirt as immoral.

5 Making contact

On contact, greet them with a friendly smile. Speak carefully and
slowly. Try not to be patronizing. Your first objective is to find
out how much English they know. This can be done by asking a
question which does not require a 'yes' or 'no' answer but rather a
sentence. Questions such as 'How long have you been in
England ?' 'Where do you come from ?' could be used. While

speaking, make a mental note of their dress and features as a guide to their religion and language. If they invite you in, this is good, as it can lead to contact with others, and also the breaking down of barriers. Most probably you will be the first European to enter their home.

If they do not speak English, produce your literature and offer it (right way up and preferably in the right language). If they do speak English, try to make friends a little before turning to literature. Children are sometimes helpful as interpreters, when their parents do not speak English.

6 *Eating and drinking in their homes*
Accept cheerfully and thankfully any food or drink that you are offered. Learn to like coffee and heavily sweetened beverages.

7 *Speaking of Christianity*
If asked who you are, try not to use the word 'Christian' as the Asian thinks that all English people are Christians. Instead try to express it differently, for example 'I am a follower of the Lord Jesus Christ and here to tell of his love'. If asked about the church, say that you represent the local church, giving its name.

Avoid using terms which may be misunderstood by the Asian, for example 'Son of God' to the Muslim, or words which may be interpreted in a different context, for example 'salvation', 'atonement', 'redemption', 'sin'. Try to express biblical truths in simple meaningful language. Do not spend much time on abstract philosophical arguments. Even though this may be enjoyable it does not lead to anything positive. A word of personal testimony is much more valuable. Talk about your personal experience of the Lord, God's presence in your life, answered prayer, guidance and so on.

8 *Treatment of the Bible*
Make sure the Bible used is not dog-eared, or heavily underlined, as Asians have great reverence for their holy books. When seated never place a Bible on the floor, or in a bag on the floor. Always handle it with the greatest of respect.

9 *Personal questions*
If personal questions are asked, answer them without embarrassment. Do not be afraid to ask personal questions in return. Withholding answers looks like lack of confidence and is treated with suspicion.

First visit

On the first visit, aim for a friendly contact rather than a theological argument. Sow seeds which can be followed up on another visit.

Subsequent visits

You may find your contacts less friendly. Women may appear afraid if the previous visit was resented by the men. It is possible that they have suspected your aims and now regard you with suspicion. Do not force the issue, but continue a friendly contact until their confidence is won.

Practical ways of helping immigrants

1 By answering questions concerning income tax forms, national health schemes, rates, special services available for immigrants, education etc.

2 By giving information on the habits, customs and culture of the British.

3 By lending a hand with practical jobs.

Aims of visitation

1 To welcome immigrants to the area.

2 To assure them of the sympathy and availability of church members in times of need and difficulty.

3 To inform them of church activities.

4 To assure them of their acceptance within the church.

5 To present the claims of the Gospel.

6 To learn from them about their problems, cultures, and way of life.

7 To assure them that some English people do care and wish to be their friends.

	Religion	Language	Likely country of origin	Examples of names*	Sex	Meanings etc. of names
Muslims	Islam	Urdu (Persian script, written right to left)	West Pakistan	Shahid	M	The name of the founder of the religion is often one of the men's names. Members of the same family may have different last names.
				Mohammed	M	
				Sadiq	M	
		Bengali	Bangladesh	Ali	M	
				Akbar	M	
				Rubia	F	
				Begum	F	
				Yakub	M	
				Sughan	F	
				Khan	M	
Hindus	Hinduism	Hindi (national language written left to right under the line) or the vernacular of the place of origin	India	Satya	F	Truth
				Prakash	M	Light
				Devi	F	Goddess
				Rama	M	A mythical hero
				Bhara,	M	India
		Gujarati	Gujarat, north of Bombay	Seeta	F	Wife of Rama
				Chandra	M	Moon
				Sumitra	F	Good friend
				Krishna	M	A mythical hero
				Patel	Surname	
Sikhs	Sikhism	Punjabi (written hanging under the line left to right)	Punjab (India) especially Jullundur District, Kenya, etc.	Singh	M	Lion. Used by all male Sikhs.
				Kaur	F	Used by all female Sikhs.

* Some of these names have now taken on the function of the surname to correspond with the British practice.

Source: Community Service Volunteers Project '71.

Resources

Tools for evangelism

A list of some of the items available for use in evangelism and in understanding the Asian and his way of life.

Films

The film 'Dust and Destiny' is available in Urdu for hire from Fact and Faith Films, 13a Northcote Road, London SW11.
'Journey into the Sky – the life of Sadhu Sundar Singh – is available in English and Hindustani from International Films, 545 Harrow Road London W10 4RH.

Literature

Scripture portions and booklets in many Asian languages are available from Scripture Gift Mission, Radstock House, 3 Eccleston Street, London SW1.
Bibles, Scripture portions etc., Gospel diglots in Urdu/English and Punjabi/English are all available from British and Foreign Bible Society, 146 Queen Victoria Street, London EC4.
A list giving details of books and booklets in Urdu, Hindi, Bengali, Gujarati, Punjabi, Marathi, Telugu and Malayalam can be obtained from the Asian Literature Department, Christian Literature Crusade, The Dean, Alresford, Hants.

Records

Records carrying Gospel messages in all Asian languages spoken in Britain are available free of charge from Gospel Recordings, Block 12E, Gloucester Trading Estate, Hucclecote, Gloucester, GL3 4AA.

Teaching material

Teaching tape on Islam, Hinduism, Sikhism and Buddhism are

available from Bible and Medical Missionary Fellowship, 352 Kennington Road, London SE11.

Cassettes and tapes, short Gospel and teaching messages for adults and children: from Mr A. J. Morling, 13 Betenson Avenue, Sevenoaks, Kent.

'Skin deep or deeper' is a cassette tape produced to help Christians get alongside Asians. Available from Echo, 415 Regency Mews, Silverdale Road, Eastbourne, Sussex.

Problem-solving sets consisting of worksheets, filmstrips and tape commentary on Hinduism, Buddhism and Islam, all intended for teenage groups: available from The Youth Department, Overseas Missionary Fellowship, Newington Green, London N16.

Filmstrips

Three filmstrips on Muslims, Sikhs and Hindus in Britain show the beliefs, doctrines and practices of the adherents of these religions who live in Britain and our approach as Christians to these religions. 'They came to Britain – the Muslims'; 'They came to Britain – the Sikhs'; and, 'They came to Britain – the Hindus' are available from 'In Contact', St. Andrews Road, London E13.

Other filmstrips on Eastern religions can be obtained from BMMF, Concordia and CMS.

Correspondence Courses

A Course on Luke's Gospel and also on 'What the Bible Teaches', especially designed for Asians in Britain, are available in the Asian languages and in English are available from 'In Contact', St. Andrews Road, London E13.

Bibliography

Anderson, J. N. D., *The World's Religions* (IVP)
Basham, *The Wonder that was India* (Fontana)
Bridges, Peter, *A Hindu family in Britain* (R.E.P.)
Bronnert, David, *Race* (Falcon)
The Christian Approach Series (Edinburgh House Series)
El Droubie, Riadh, *Islam* (Ward Lock Educational)
Hill, Clifford, *Immigration and Integration* (Pergamon)
Holmes, Thomas J., *Almost all Welcome* (Lakeland)
Holroyde, Peggy, *East comes West* (Community Relations Commission)
Judd, *Towards Understanding the Muslim* (CMS)
Judd, *Towards Understanding the Hindu* (CMS)
Judd, *Towards Understanding the Buddhist* (CMS)
King, Martin Luther, *Strength to Love* (Fontana)
Lalvani, *Beyond No One's Reach* (Guru Nanak Foundation)
Mason, Philip, *Race Relations* (O.U.P.)
Oakley, Robin, *New Backgrounds* (S.C.M.)
Sharma, Ursula, *Rampal and his Family* (Collins)
Skinner, Tom, *Black and Free* (Paternoster)
Stanton, *The Teaching of the Quran* (S.P.C.K.)
Wood, W. and Downing, J., *Vicious Circle* (S.P.C.K.)
'New Community', a monthly magazine from the Community Relations Commission.